BECAUSE THE LORD IS MY SHEPHERD

BECAUSE THE LORD IS MY SHEPHERD

PSALM 23 AND ME

CAROLYN BOOKER-PIERCE

Copyright © 2020 J Merrill Publishing, Inc.

All rights reserved. No part of this publication may be reproduced, distributed, or transmitted in any form or by any means, including photocopying, recording, or other electronic or mechanical methods, without the prior written permission of the publisher, except in the case of brief quotations embodied in critical reviews and certain other noncommercial uses permitted by copyright law. For permission requests, write to the publisher, addressed "Attention: Permissions Coordinator," at the address below.

ISBN: 978-1-950719-44-0 (Paperback)
ISBN: 978-1-950719-45-7 (eBook)

J Merrill Publishing, Inc.
434 Hillpine Drive
Columbus, OH 43207

www.JMerrillPublishingInc.com

This book is dedicated to my mother, Mary E. Booker, who I watched work harder than I probably ever will. It is not because I am lazy; I am just blessed to live in a time, whereas I don't have to do the taxing job of leaving my home to go clean another's home.

Sometimes she would leave one home and go to another home to clean. The Shepherd gave her the grace for that. He also gave that same grace to all the other women of her day that needed to work outside the home to help their husbands meet the needs of their back then large families.

My mother was a trooper. She gave birth to seven children; I am her fourth born.

I know it had to be someone greater than her taking care of her and watching over her as she took a bus to another part of the city into the suburbs to clean houses.

I am forever grateful to God for how he took care of my mother. I am forever grateful to my mother for how she did her best to watch over me. I also thank those who have encouraged me in writing and releasing this book: my sister Jennifer, my friends Karen, Shawn, two Cheryl's. Yes, I am blessed with two Cheryl's in my life as friends.

Some encouraged, while some inspired me to write again. Still, others looked over my book, checked my terrible spelling, and prayed for me as I struggled to believe I could write anything worth reading. I am truly grateful for my family, friends, and readers of this book.

Thanks for supporting me when you did not have to. You know who you are.
Most importantly, I know who you are.

CONTENTS

Introduction	ix
1. My Shepherd Takes Care of Me	1
2. My Shepherd Teaches Me How To Rest	19
3. My Shepherd Heals My Mind	31
4. My Shepherd Is With Me, I Shall Not Be Afraid	39
5. What Do You Do With Your Enemies?	55
6. Goodness and Mercy Will Follow You	63
About the Author	77
Also by Carolyn Booker-Pierce	79

INTRODUCTION

Are there times when you feel like you are out there on your own? It may seem like there is no one out there to help you but you. There is not even one person who sees that you need help. Even if they saw you, they could not help you.

Well, let me share some of my experiences with Psalm 23. Let me share some of my experiences with the good Shepherd. I named this book's subtitle Psalm 23 and me because it is personal. I am writing out of my own experience with Psalm 23.

Oh, let me put out this disclaimer before you read my book. I don't consider myself to be a professional when it comes to book writing. Still, I do consider myself an expert when it comes to depending on and trusting in God.

I have been in the school of the Shepherd for a long time. I grew up hearing Psalm 23 in churches, quoted by my elders, and I have seen all kinds of plaques with the famous chapter written on it. It always made me feel good when I first started reading it for myself.

However, over the years, it has become a real connection to who I believe God is to me. I did not really start meditating on what it said until I found myself feeling like a lost sheep. It was then I began to identify with the Lord as being a shepherd. The more problems or tests I found myself in, the more I read Psalm 23.

As I read, I understood how the Lord earned Shepherd as one of his names. Psalm 23 had started to become more personal to me.

It became more than just a lovely Psalm

that David wrote that people like to quote. It was personal. It had become a psalm for me.

It became a reality about how a good shepherd cares for his sheep. In caring for their sheep, shepherds would help sheep stay out of trouble or lead them when they got into trouble. I am one of those sheep that was always getting into trouble. I am one of those sheep that the Shepherd has had to rescue.

Are you one of those sheep? Are you a person that, although you try to live right every day you find yourself wandering off away from the fold? Are you a 'good person' that sometimes life will land in unforeseen circumstances that only a good shepherd can get you out of?

You may love the Lord, your Shepherd, and he loves you too, but every sheep needs a shepherd. Why, because we don't know everything.

I have learned that sheep are not very smart. I have learned that I am not very smart compared to my Shepherd. I have learned that I don't have to know everything. I just need to know the Shepherd because he takes good care of me. He knows how to take good care of you.

I hope you are encouraged by my experience of being led by the Lord. Because the Lord is my Shepherd, he takes good care of me. Like I said, it is personal.

> PSALM 23 (KJV)
> The LORD is my Shepherd; I shall not want.
> 2 He maketh me to lie down in green pastures: he leadeth me beside the still waters.
> 3 He restoreth my soul: he leadeth me in the paths of righteousness for his name's sake.
> 4 Yea, though I walk through the valley of the shadow of death, I will fear no evil: for thou art with me; thy rod and thy staff they comfort me.
> 5 Thou preparest a table before me in the presence of mine enemies: thou anointest my

head with oil; my cup runneth over.

6 Surely goodness and mercy shall follow me all the days of my life: and I will dwell in the house of the LORD for ever.

1

MY SHEPHERD TAKES CARE OF ME

The LORD is my Shepherd; I shall not want.
Psalm 1:1

What is a shepherd or sheepherder? It is a person who tends to, feeds, or guard herds of sheep. A shepherd takes care of sheep. That is what the Lord is to me. I am one of his sheep.

Did you know sheep are considered dumb? They don't know everything and tend to get lost. They sometimes wander off and find themselves in danger. Therefore, they need a shepherd to lead and guide them. That is why the Lord is considered to be a shepherd, a good shepherd at that. He is my Shepherd, and he takes good care of me. He not only takes care of me; he will take care of everything that concerns me.

> *The LORD will perfect that which concerneth me*
> *Psalms 138:8*

That means He will take care of all of those that belong to him. The Lord tends to my needs making sure I am being fed both spiritually and physically. He guides me, guards me, and he watches over me to protect me. My Shepherd supplies all of my needs.

When I think of how I watched over my children, tending to them, raising them, feeding them, guiding them, and protecting them, it gives me a good picture of how my Shepherd takes care of and watches over me.

As a mother, I made sure my children were fed every day, they had warm clothes, and they had comfortable beds to sleep in. My children were protected from strangers by me locking doors, and they were never left alone to fend for themselves, as children.

I always looked out for them. They did not want for anything. They may have said they wanted certain things, but as a mother, I knew what they needed. Therefore, I gave them whatever they needed, just like my Shepherd knows exactly what I need. He always gives me that which I need. If there is something the Lord does not give me, I think of three things; (1) I did not need it, (2) it was not the right time for it, or (3) it would cause me harm to receive it. It is up to my Shepherd to decide.

In any case, I am never in want or in need. I remember wanting to move out of my parent's home for the first time. I had never lived on my own. It would be a big step for me, not knowing where I would live or how much I would end up paying for rent. The first thing I did was pray to the Lord, my Shepherd. I had read enough scripture to know and believe the Lord, my Shepherd, would meet all my needs. Last I check it is still written in Philippians 4:19.

But my God shall supply all your need according to his riches in glory by Christ Jesus.

I can remember looking in the daily newspaper under rentals and apartments. I had a certain price range I wanted to stay within. I was a single mother with other bills to pay. As I combed through the paper, I saw a duplex that caught my attention. It was in the area I wanted to live in, check. It was in the price range I wanted to pay, check. Then I saw approval based on a credit check, not checked. I had not checked my credit report because that was something at the time I did not think about or wanted to think about. I knew my credit score might not be good. I knew I was late on my last one or two car payments earlier that year due to recently coming off of maternity leave. I did mention I was a single mother at the time. But God, in His mercy, sent His son to die for my sin and mistakes he knew I would make. Children are a gift from God, but I did not wait until I was married. The good shepherd did not judge me; he forgave me. Remember, because the Lord is my Shepherd, he takes care of me.

Well, I stepped out on faith and called the number of the renter of the duplex. She set a time for me to meet with her at the duplex. I got there on time. I saw the duplex and immediately fell in love with it. It had just enough room for me and my little family. The bathroom was newly remodeled with a beautiful Hollywood style bathroom. I loved the bathroom and the duplex. Then came the questions,

Landlord: "How do you like the place?"

Me: "I love the place. It is perfect."

Landlord: "Do you have your deposit and the first month's rent?"

Me: With a smile on my face, "Yes, I do."

Landlord: Do you have the $25.00 to fill out the application for the credit report?'

Me: With hesitation, "Yes, I do."

Landlord: "You will occupy the bottom duplex, and my sister will be living above you."

Me: "That is fine."

Landlord: "You and my sister will share a basement. One side yours the other side hers."

Me: "That is fine."

Landlord: "You seem like a nice person. I am going to skip the credit report and just take your deposit and rent if you are ready to move in."

Me: "Yes, thank you. I appreciate that. I will pay you on time."

Me: Speaking to myself, "Thank you, Lord. I know that was you."

The Lord, my Shepherd, had guided me to the right renter that day. He provided for me and protected me from what may have been a bad credit report stopping my family from having housing we needed.

I had a need, but I was not left wanting. My Shepherd took good care of me one of his sheep that day. I was saved from want. I also saved $25.00 that would have been spent on a credit report. I was saved from embarrassment if a report would have come back negative.

That day will always be a reminder for me that the Lord, my Shepherd, would supply my needs for housing. One year later, I wanted to move to a bigger place. I was over my cute one-floor duplex. I was running out of space. I thought a townhome would be more spacious. I began my search. I found the perfect townhome and neighborhood for me and my family. I had paid my rent on time for the whole year, but I still had not checked my credit report. I put my application in by faith, remembering what the good Shepherd had done the year before.

Well, I talked myself right out of faith. I had put in my application for the townhouse, which included a credit report. I was told by the rental office staff that I would get a call within a couple of days. A couple of days had come and gone. It had been a couple of weeks, three weeks, to be exact. When I did not hear back from the rental office, I assumed the credit report came back with a bad score despite my efforts to redeem my credit. I did not call them.

I had resolved I would stay at the duplex another year, renewing a lease that I did not want to renew. The gas bill of the cute little duplex was $500.00 a month during the winter due to the high ceilings. I was paying almost twice the amount I was paying for rent. That was back in the early eighties. I doubt that one could find something as cute as the duplex for 225.00 today.

There I was, ready to stay another year. I had not contacted the townhome rental office for fear that I was denied. However, this is how my Shepherd showed his sense of humor.

A tiny little mouse showed up running around in my cute one-floor space duplex. I was terrified. The little gray mouse with a pink nose had me standing in the middle of my bed, crying for help. I had contacted my father to ask him to come over and get rid of the little mouse that was holding me hostage.

His remarks were "that mouse is probably scared of you. I am not coming. I am going to work." With that, he hung up on me. I was mortified. I threw things at the mouse, and the mouse just stood on the floor, staring at me like I was a crazy person. Looking back, it was crazy for me being this giant-size creature screaming over a ball of fur that I should have had the guts to stomp on.

In any case, I had to decide due to the fact I had a job to go to, and the mouse was not moving. As soon as I jumped down to bolt to the restroom, the little ball of fur took off running too.

After work that day, I went to a hardware store and purchased some mouse traps. I set them as the man in the store instructed. Then one day, there it was. The furry little guy was stuck to the trap, but I immediately thought, "I am not touching that gross looking creature."

For years I thought my son took the mouse out after I asked him to dispose of the furry guy. He recently told me he asked one of the boys in the neighborhood to take it out. I was giving the family my fear of a mouse. In my heart, I was sensing I was supposed to contact the townhome rental office, but I was too afraid of being denied. I had forgotten about how my good Shepherd had taken care of me the last time I was ready to move, especially when I did not hear back from the rental office.

Then something more frightening happened. I left for work one day, turning off all the lights, locking up the house as I always had done. However, while I was at work and the children at school, someone had broken into my duplex, my home, my children's home. To my surprise, nothing was taken. However, I noticed I had this touch lamp that would come on with just a jar of sound by itself. I had turned the light off before leaving for work that morning. I examined the house to see if the money that was left in a top drawer was missing; it was not. I further checked out the house. Nothing was missing. The only thing I found disturbed was a side door that had been broken down by whoever had gotten in. Then I looked over at the lamp that I had turned off when I left home that morning. It was now on.

All I could come up with was when whoever broke into my or busted in the door, the lamp came on, scaring them away. The lamp would be right in the view of the door that was broken. After the break-in, all of a sudden, I felt an urgency to move out as fast as I could.

Something told me (the Holy Spirit) to call to check on the application for the townhome

I had applied for three weeks prior. One of the rental office staff answered the phone. When I asked what the status of the application was, the staff began offering me an apology. She said she thought she had called me to tell me I had been approved three weeks before, right after I had applied. She continued to apologize, saying that the townhome was still available if I wanted it, and I could move in as soon as the new carpet was laid. I quickly told her I still wanted the townhome, and I thanked her, for I was so ready to move. You see, my Shepherd was taking care of me.

When it was time for me to move, He allowed the gas bill to increase, the mouse to invade my space, and a thief to break in while protecting me and my children. He protected me by not allowing the thief to take anything. Now my need for another home was met because my Shepherd took care of me. Another lesson I learned that His word is true in Romans chapter 8.

And we know that All things work together for good to them that

*love God, to them who are the
called according to his purpose*
Romans 8:28 KJV

After moving into the townhome about three years later, I started having car trouble. You would think by now I would not be afraid of credit reports. To be honest, I was not as smart financially, then like I am now. However, here I go again, trusting that the Lord, my Shepherd, would be with me to meet the need for a new car.

I went to a car dealership with exactly 89 cents in my pocket. I remember thinking, I either had a lot of faith, or I was just plum crazy. I walked into the dealership just to check out some cars and prices. I was not expecting to come out with a brand new car that day or that month. I was still trying to find a buyer for my old car. It still ran, but I was not a mechanic, and I knew that I would be putting more money in the car to keep it running.

Here comes the good old salesman. He had no idea I had only 89 cents in my pocket. I was not about to tell him. His only goal was to sell me a car anyway he can. He began to tell me how much he wanted to put me in a brand new car. I wanted to tell him that I really can't afford an old car, let alone a new car. But, I kept the faith and let the salesman show me a new car. It was not just any car. It was the car that I wanted but felt like I could not afford it. I saw the car. I drove the car. I loved the car. I was so excited I had forgotten I only had 89 cents in my pocket.

The salesman realized how excited I was about the car. He stopped his pitch and invited me into his cubicle area. He started quoting the prices, payments, and interest. I had totally fallen into the shepherd arms. I needed him to pick me up and take over. It was like I was in a fog. Then here comes the thing that usually sends me into fear, the credit report application. However, I sat there like a person with good credit. I prayed God if you have to do something to the credit score system so that I will have good credit, please do it now. I want this car. The salesman had me sign the consent to run the credit check. He walked out of the cubicle for what seemed like an eternity. Then he comes back, walking really fast like with excitement. This is what he said, "you have excellent credit!"

I wanted to fall out of the chair and ask him who has excellent credit, but I kept my mouth shut, afraid to open it. He went on to say that I could buy any car on the lot. Now it did not take a rocket scientist for me to know how my credit report came back excellent. I knew it was the Good Shepherd taking care of me. Remember, I walked in with 89 cents and probably a low credit score. Next thing I know, I am walking out with a new car and a new credit score. Yes, because the Lord is my Shepherd, that is what He has done for me.

By the way, I did not know how I was going to pay for this new car, but the good Shepherd did. A couple of weeks later, the good Shepherd blessed me with two raises back to back. One was an annual raise, and the other was for a reclassification I had put in for months before and had forgotten about. It was approved with back pay. Before I had prayed, he had answered me. I just needed to step out on faith because the Lord, my Shepherd, would again supply all my needs. I can truly say like Paul in Philippians 4:19, "My God shall supply all your needs."

When it came time for me to buy my first house, I had plenty of practice having faith in the good Shepherd. I looked and looked and looked for a house. I had a price range in mind that I did not want to exceed. Every house that I was interested in was way above the price range I felt the Lord had told me to stay in. One day I was tired of looking. I told the realtor I was done looking. The realtor said I have just one more house I want you to see before you quit. The price of the house was just lowered to my price range that day. She said, please, would you take a look at this one house? She said it has everything on your wish list. Of course, you know what happened. I walked into the house, and I immediately knew it was my house. I was standing in the house that seemed to take so long to find. It was the house the good Shepherd had lowered just for me. The owner was trying to move into a senior living home and was tired of waiting on a buyer. Therefore lowered the price that day. On the day I felt I was done with looking for a house was the day I found my house. I felt in my heart the house was lowered just for me. I will never forget that house. It was my first home. It had everything I wanted, including a kitchen table and chair set and a queen bed the seller sold me for $100.00. I remember there was a built-in dining cabinet that matched the pattern of my dining room table and chair set I already had.

Wow, what a confirmation. Just when I thought it was not time for the Shepherd to meet my need, he showed up with bells and whistles. He was saying to me I am here, my sheep. I am here to meet your need. My second home went sort of the same way. When I finally found the house, I walked in and knew that was it. I had been looking for a while again. There was a time I just stopped looking. But when it was time, there was an even bigger blessing attached to it that made me glad I had to wait. Do you remember when President Obama issued the first-time home buyers $8000.00 tax-free credit? The credit was offered to help encourage people to buy homes that had not been selling at the time? You guessed it. I got in on that. If I had found a home prior to the release of that credit, I would have missed earning the tax-free $8000.00 credit check. It was unexpected, but such a blessing at the time. You never know why the Shepherd sometimes says wait, but he still promises to meet all of our needs. Therefore don't give up. His answer still may be no but wait. I got something better. Just know that a good shepherd will take care of, tend to, guard, and protect his sheep. His sheep shall not want or be in need because the Lord is our Shepherd.

2

MY SHEPHERD TEACHES ME HOW TO REST

> He maketh me to lie down in green pastures:
> he leadeth me beside the still waters
> *Psalm 23:2*

Do you know how to rest? What is that? Sometimes I don't know what it is or how to obtain it. I can be sitting still at home with nothing to do, but my mind refuses to shut out the noise—the noise of what I should be doing or still have not done. Things, if I think about it, can wait until tomorrow. I don't always know how to rest. While sitting still, I will start thinking of a bill

I want to pay off, some work in the house that needs to be done (nothing urgent), or just somewhere I think I should be going. Actually, I think I start feeling guilty when I try to rest or relax. Therefore my mind starts looking for something to do. Why can't I just be still and do nothing? Why can't I try to be quit from all the noise in my head and just relax? Why can't I let the peace of God give me the rest I need? Do you have that problem?

What usually happens when I forget to rest, or I just keep going without peace, my body and my mind have a way of letting me know. I start feeling really tired or sometimes just downright exhausted. I start getting confused. If you ask my children, they think it is just mom being confused because she is getting older. That could be true, too, due to the fact I forget more things now than I did in the past. In any case, I usually can tell when I am not getting enough rest or not allow myself to rest in God. That is not good for me. That is not good for the people around me. That is not good for anything I need to be responsible for. I work in a profession where I am trained to help others take care of themselves. You would think I would take better care of myself and rest often. If you are in a profession of helping people, you know like I know how to take care of yourself, but we do not always do it. If you are like me, are a social worker, nurse, doctor, minister of the gospel, or any type of caregiver, you know how hard it is not to allow people and things to come before God.

I came in the New Year, declaring my own personal self- care would be my number one goal. I pride myself on having a health coach to help me meet that goal. By the middle of the year, I started to notice I was failing royally with my self-care goal. Sure at the beginning of the year, I was exercising, eating healthier, praying, and meditating. I was taking at least one day out of the week to do nothing but whatever I enjoyed doing that is relaxing. That consisted of hanging out with one of my close friends for a movie, lunch, and laughs. Or I would plan something for me and my adorable spoiled grandson.

I don't know how in the world he became

so spoiled. Do you have any idea? And yes, I am being sarcastic, but others have contributed to him being tremendously spoiled, not just my contribution. However, he brings me joy and warms my heart by saying all the things a grandparent would want to hear from a precious grandchild. He's a certified charmer. Then life continued to happen as it always does. I started writing this book in 2016. At the time, I had a 40-hour a week job, two parents I was trying to protect from the nursing home system, church, a failing marriage, and things around the house that needed attention—all of which I needed, and they needed me. Since I honor and take pride in serving them all, I finally found myself struggling to find rest. All of which is important to me. However, I needed to be important to me.

That is how I found myself asking these questions. Where is the Psalm 1:2 rest? Where are the green pastures? Surely if David was made to lie down in green pastures and was led beside the still waters, so can I. Well, the day came. I was made to lie down I mean literally laid down. The green pastures I am referring to is called my bed. I was made to lie down at home where I drug myself to bed after a meltdown that I could not control. My memory was leaving fast, I was becoming confused, I became easily frustrated, and the tears were flowing at a drop a hat. I knew what was happening. I know the signs of burnout and the feelings of being overwhelmed. I have been there before. Like most people who just have the heart to help others and see them do well and get better, we forget to put our mask on first. Yes, just like they tell you on the airplane. Put your mask on first; then you can help others. We forget to take care of ourselves or put God first (Matthew 6:33). It is not deliberate. We just become so focused on trying to help others we sometimes miss a step, asking God for help and taking care of ourselves. If we would only put the mask on first as instructed on the airplane, we would not lose air. If I am losing air, I will pass out and not be able to help myself or the person I am trying to help.

There I was falling asleep while trying to

watch the evening news with a bottle of water to quench my thirst. I was so tired I didn't want to eat. I didn't have time to think about eating. Fixing a meal was not even on my radar. That was happening more and more. What was on my radar had become sleep. I just need to go to sleep. I felt myself shutting down. The plan every day once I got home was to get in my PJ's as fast as I could. However, sleep beat me to it. I was made to lie down in green pastures. I was made to lie beside the still waters. It was more like passing out in the green pastures. Green pastures are created to enjoy not for passing out in. I should have taken better care of myself, my body, mind, and spirit. I was drained. I had been saying I need a vacation, but it appeared life events would not allow it. What was interesting was getting up every morning asking God to please help me. I was waking up with back pain, no energy, and feeling like a ton of bricks. God was telling me in my spirit to lie down and rest. I thought that meant to rest only for one day. However, my idea of rest and His were two different things. Matthew 11:28 NIV says,

Come unto me, all you who are weary and burdened, and I will give rest.

It took back pain, being so tired I could not eat, crying at the drop of a hat and falling asleep while watching the evening news for me to go to bed. It was like everything came to a stop. He made me lie down in green pastures, and he led me beside the still waters (the work of God). He gave me rest. He made me lay down. I had to turn to Him, the good Shepherd, to get back up.

> *Take my yoke upon you and learn from me, for I am gentle and humble in heart, and you will find rest for your souls. For my yoke is easy and my burden is light."*
> *Matthew 11:29-30*

When we submit ourselves to Christ, we also free ourselves from the yoke of bondage created in this world. The yoke of the world is burdensome. It will make you think you have to do what only the Shepherd can do. The yoke connected with the world is hard but being yoked to Jesus Christ (Yeshua the Messiah) makes life easy. It is a rest for those who have been weighed down by the sins and cares of the world. It is a rest for those who carry false burdens. That is a burden of taking care of something that God should be taking care of or is not an assignment for you. It is a burden that needs to be laid down so you can rest. When getting into eternal rest, you will be freed from those heavy burdens weighing you down. We come into the world of unrest, but Jesus came to give us rest. I have learned to check my relationship with the Father, the good Shepherd. If my relationship with him is falling off, then I tend to lose rest. That is when I need to slow down and return to him. If you have found your relationship with the good Shepherd has fallen, get back in a relationship. Pray, read your Bible, meditate on scripture for only He can give you rest. The good Shepherd offers rest to those who have been struggling with a relationship apart from Him.

Before coming to Christ, I struggled because I was trying to do things in my own strength. I did not know how much I needed help. I did not know how to rest or that there was somewhere I could go to find rest. In April 1978, I was introduced to that soul-saving rest. I was tired. I had been laboring and heavy laden for a while. But when I yoked up with the good Shepherd, I learned of him, that he was meek and lowly in heart towards me, and I found rest for my soul (mind, will, and emotions). It was then I was able to turn everything over to him, including my life. It was a life that consisted of worldly living. I was up late at night. I hung around the wrong people, and the wrong people hung around me. I was a single mother worrying that I would not be able to be a good parent for my child. At the time, I had not finished high school. I was still making a lot of bad choices. But when I yoked up with the good Shepherd, things got better. I did not have to do things alone then, and I don't have to do things alone now. I had help from the savior, the good Shepherd. He had begun to guide me into a new way of living, a new way of thinking, and a new way of rest.

My mind (my soul) began to rest. My body began to heal. My soul found peace. My soul was resting from all of the things that were out of control. I now have help from the Father, his Son, and the Holy Spirit. I now have wisdom that came not from the world but from above. I know I have eternal rest for my soul. That is a rest that will always be there. However, if I am not careful, I will forget I have that rest. I may forget to use the rest and wisdom that allows me to tap into that supernatural peace the Shepherd offers me because the Lord is my Shepherd. He takes good care of me.

Christ, the savior, believed in getting away to a quiet place after dealing with people all day. He would teach and heal the multitudes. He was God in the flesh, manifesting God's glory to men and women daily. His body got tired. He went without food caring for the people he ministered to, his disciples following him too. He finally addresses their fatigue in Mark.

> *Then, because so many people were coming and going that they did not even have a chance to eat, he said to them, "Come with me by yourselves to a quiet place and get some rest."*
> Mark 6:31

As much as Jesus loved healing the sick and ministering to the people he knew when it was time to rest. He told the disciples to come with him by themselves. Don't bring anyone with you. He encouraged them to go to a quiet place, away from the crowd, away from the noise so they could rest.

Do you sometimes feel like you need to get away to a quiet place, away from the crowd, away from people, away from the noise of life, and just rest? I do. Today I don't have any problem when I am tired of getting away by myself to a quiet place and getting some rest. It is in those times if you follow the Shepherd, he will give you rest.

A nice vacation will not hurt anybody. However, you may not be able to pack up and head to the beach. The psalmist says He maketh me to lie down in green pastures can you picture how peaceful the green pasture of a field looks clothed in the beauty of God? Even more peaceful are still waters (being with the Father). The fresh air that flows off of the still waters or being still at the water (he is that water), he can restore your soul. I can see myself at the beach right now, located at a nice hotel where I don't have to do anything but relax. That is my natural idea of getting away for rest. However, I can't always physically be at the beach where I can rest, but my spirit can rest by just being still and being quiet in the presence of the Shepherd. Sometimes that is all it takes to rest, just being still resting in God.

3

MY SHEPHERD HEALS MY MIND

He restoreth my soul: he leadeth me in the paths of righteousness for his name's sake
Psalm 23:3

When God created man, He created man in his image Genesis 1:26a, "And God said, Let us make man in our image, after our likeness:" Man, both male and female, was created by the God of the trinity in a triune way meaning in three parts; body, soul and spirit. Another reference to man being triune is in 1 Thessalonians 5:23,

And the very God of peace sanctify you wholly; I pray God your whole spirit and soul and body be preserved blameless unto the coming of our Lord Jesus Christ (KJV).

To think we are only physical beings is dangerous due to what happens to man once he or she dies. If we were only physical beings, we would die, and that would be the end of it. However, due to man being created in body (physical), soul (mind, will, and emotions) and spirit (which is closely related to the mind however not the same), one should recognize all three parts of man as God has created and purposed. If then our being is three parts most would understand what happens to the body when it dies, it returns to dust. Since man is more than a body, and according to the word, he is a living soul. The Bible says,

And the Lord God formed man of

> *the dust of the ground, and breathed into his nostrils the breath of life, and man became a living soul"*
> Genesis 2:7

What is the soul of man? The soul of man is what operates through our minds, such as our imagination, conscience, memory, reasoning, and the affections. Because the soul is a natural part of man, not spiritual, thoughts, imaginations and conscience, reasoning, memory, and affections can become damaged, broken, or misconstrued. Thus the soul needs to be restored and renewed. Our natural man (soul) has a way of causing our thoughts to be shattered, not lining up with the mind of Christ if not renew. Therefore we are encouraged to renew our mind in Romans chapter 12,

> *And be not conformed to this world: but be ye transformed by the renewing of your mind,*

> *that ye may prove what is*
> *that good, and acceptable, and*
> *perfect, will of God*
> Romans 12:2 KJV).

Depending on what happens in our lives, and depending on the choices we make here on earth, one could end up with a lost or damaged soul. If one is not given the wisdom of God by way of the word of God and the Holy Spirit and chooses not to serve the creator who knows how to give rest. That person is subject to have soul (mind, will, and emotional) problems. If we are not willing to give our lives to the one who can save our lives, we cause our own destructive thinking. Therefore we allow ourselves to be destroyed if we are not led by the spirit.

> *For what man knoweth the things*
> *of a man, save the spirit of*
> *man which is in him? Even so*
> *the things of God knoweth no*
> *man, but the Spirit of God*
> *1 Corinthians 2:9-11 KJV*

In David's case, he had gone through a time that could have destroyed him mentally. David had sinned against God, but he could gladly say He restoreth my soul. By the grace of God, David was able to keep his sanity and be led back to God when he wandered away from God. Remember, I said earlier; sheep tend to be dumb. Sheep tend to wander. David did not lose his mind because the Lord, his Shepherd, was constantly watching over him and ready to restore his soul when David repented. David sinned with Bathsheba that cost him his child. However, after David turned to the good Shepherd crying out for forgiveness, he was forgiven. David goes on to say what happened next,

> *He leadeth me in the paths of righteousness for his name's sake (3b).*

God not only restored David's soul; he restored his wandering mind leading him in the path of right living for his name's sake.

What an awesome thing to happen after

committing sin and being forgiven. We all have sinned, according to Roman 3:23. David's sin was that he committed adultery with another man's wife. He went a step further, killing the husband of the woman he slept with. While he came with a hefty price to pay, David still saw God for who he is, a good shepherd leading his lost sheep back to the fold.

David knew first-hand how a shepherd cared for his sheep. He, himself, was a shepherd that tended sheep. He knew how sheep could be dumb and wander off, getting themselves into trouble. He knew how he loved his sheep, took care of his sheep, and would rescue them. He especially knew how to take care of them after they had been attacked as a result of them wandering off and leaving the fold. He would not leave them. He would restore them to the fold.

I have been there and done that. I have wandered off, making bad decisions. Some were so bad that I thought I would lose my mind (soul), but the same Shepherd that rescued and restore David rescued and restored me. The same Shepherd that led David in the path of righteousness reached out his loving arms and led me back on the path of righteousness.

I have put myself in some situations I did not know how I was going to get out of. There were times I could not eat and could not sleep. I had become so broken and torn because of the messes I had created. However, God, for his name's sake, would not leave me alone broken, torn, and lost. He rescued me, and he restored my soul (mind, will, and emotions). He led me back on the path of righteousness, making his way perfect again. Therefore, I can sing praises like David sung unto the Lord, his Shepherd.

> *As for God, his way is perfect; the word of the LORD is tried: he is a buckler to all them that trust in him. For who is God, save the LORD? and who is a rock, save our God. God is my*

strength and power: and he maketh my way perfect,
2 Samuel 22:31-33.

4

MY SHEPHERD IS WITH ME, I SHALL NOT BE AFRAID

Yea, though I walk through the valley of the shadow of death, I will fear no evil: for thou art with me; thy rod and thy staff they comfort me
Psalm 23:4

Have you ever been afraid? I have terribly afraid due to several near-death experiences. If you can relate, you will understand what I am about to share. When I was a youngster, it was not unusual for my siblings and I to visit the neighborhood swimming pool. I knew I could not swim, but the opportunity to hang out with family and friends was a great pass time for a hot summer day. Plus, I was not about to stay home and be left behind. One of those hot summer days, I was hanging around the shallow water, maybe two to three feet deep. A family friend's ideal of fun was pulling me way out into the deeper water, knowing that I could not swim. I was terrified because I knew I could not swim. He dragged me out into the deep water, I panicked, and you know the rest of the story. I started fighting against the water, inhaling the water that set me into the motion of choking and near-drowning. The family friend laughed and enjoyed watching me as I literally fought for my life.

To this day, I do not remember how I got out of the water, but a spirit of fear set in that would have me paralyzed when it came to water for years. After that day, I did not go swimming much, especially when the family friend was joining us. I was good at not going out into the deep water, and I was good with not being able to swim. I felt I was accomplishing what I had gone to the pool for cooling off.

Years later, as an act of faith, I sat out to go back into the water at a hotel swimming pool with other friends and family. I had a child that could swim at this point in my life. I had learned how to float a little that helped me to branch out a little further than the three feet of water. However, I never liked going in where the water was past my neck or above my head. I was out in the water floating and feeling pretty comfortable. I happened to glance over at the feet of water written inside of the pool. I saw nine feet on the wall of the pool, and immediately fear and panic set in again. I started trying to swim back to the other side of the pool. In my fear of, I found myself experiencing the same situation that I had experienced years earlier when I was pulled into deep water. Only this time, I had floated into nine feet of water, and when I tried to stand up, I could not. I had drifted too far out, and of course, my feet could not touch the bottom. I continued fighting the water, trying to get out just getting the same results as the last time. I started drowning.

I thought I was going to die. Since I had floated around in the water for a long time without incident, my family and friends thought I was playing. I could hear them saying, "look at Carolyn. She is playing like she is drowning." This group was not the same as those around during the time of my first near-drowning experience. Therefore I was in trouble. I was looking Death in the face, again. I feared I was going to die because no one was aware of the fact I was not playing. I was drowning. I was getting tired from fighting the water. Finally, by God's grace, it became apparent to one of my friends that I was drowning. He jumped in the water and got me out before I died in the water. I don't think I prayed. I don't think I had nothing on my mind other than I was going to die while others watched and laughed. The only difference between those laughing this time and the person laughing the other time, they didn't know I was not playing. But God did. He knew I was in trouble. He knew like a dumb sheep I had wandered off into deep water. He knew I was facing death. I love Psalms 91 there. I find so many good promises. One of the promises is found in verse 15,

I will be with him in trouble; I
will rescue him" (NASB).

That is what happened for the second time when I was faced with dying; God rescued me. In the shadow of death, I lived because the Lord is my Shepherd, and he saved me.

After that near-drowning incident, I again stayed out of the swimming pools for a long time. Years down the road after I had really come to know Christ as my savior, as my rescuer, I knew that God did not want me to be afraid of dying or the shadow of death. He reminds me even though I was out there in deep waters, he did not let me drown. Even though life events caused me to land in deep waters, I did not drown. He rescued me.

I decided to take the beginner's swimming

lessons at the YWCA. My goal was to eliminate the fear of swimming.

I thought I would learn how to swim in the 6 foot and be done with it. Mind you, it was a "beginners" class. The first sessions I thought went well. I was learning to swim on top of the water. I was swimming in the 6 foot, but I was not interested in anything higher. Towards the last couple of weeks of the class, I was getting comfortable with the progress I had made. I would swim on my stomach, and on my back, I thought I was ready for the Olympics. Then one day, the instructor asked me to meet him on the other end of the pool. I knew the other end of the pool was the 12-foot area. I knew because as comfortable as I was getting, I stayed away from the really deep water. I felt myself starting to get anxious, but I also knew the only way to overcome the fear of deep, over that shadow, was to get in it. I knew I would be safe, whatever was about to happen. I had built up some trust with the instructor, and my faith had increased in God, the good Shepherd that watches over me.

The instructor informed me to complete

the beginner's class I needed to swim across the 12 feet of water. He must have since the fear by the look on my face. I have never been good at having a poker face. I wanted him to know how terrified I was. He did, and he began to reassure me that he was going to be watching me, walking alongside the pool as I went across to make sure I would not drown. He said I first needed to stand at the edge of the pool and just jump straight in feet-first. He promised me I would float back up to the top. At his word that he would jump straight in and rescue me if I got in trouble, I jumped. Isn't that just like God? When he sees we are in trouble or that we are drowning, he will jump in and rescue us. Now, he will not jump in if we are swimming with a cut finger or a bad headache. We can do just fine floating with that. He knows he has to let us learn how to swim in the shallow waters and how to live. He also knows when we are facing death versus the shadow, or our imagination, of death. Sometimes we think we are going to drown, but it is just our imagination due to the waves that life sometimes brings us.

When it is just a wave he is not coming in, he will let us go through it. Well, I did not drown. I jumped in, and I came back up, just like the instructor said. He had me do that several times so that I could build trust that the water would naturally bring me up, and I would not drown. Then he told me it was time to swim across the 12 feet of water. He again reassured me he would be right along the edge until I reach the other side. That was comforting because I knew he would be able to see me if I needed to be rescued. Also, I was able to see his shadow from the pool as I swim across, not the shadow of death of which I feared.

One thing I learned from the almost death experiences, even though it looked like I was going to die, I felt like I was going to die, his rod and staff comforted me. My Shepherd would reach down and rescued me if I was in trouble. Later in life, I continued to have other valley experiences. I had valleys of sickness and valleys of hard times. I came to understand that the valleys were just valleys I had to go through. The shadows were only shadows that would not take me out because of my

Shepherd watching over me. I learned even in my worst situation, like his word says, thou are there, yes He was always there to protect me and comfort me. I have survived cancer, which should have been a scary thing. However, during the time I was diagnosed, I was not afraid.

His rod and his staff comforted me. In my spirit, I sensed I would be alright. Maybe it was how I came to know I had cancer. This is my cancer story? It was in the early 1980s I was sitting in a church service one day. My pastor at the time had just returned to the pulpit for the first time after having a heart attack and heart surgery. In his testimony of how God delivered him from his shadow of death, he urged the congregation always to have yearly checkups or a physical. He said we might be able to prevent what happened to him if we just have a checkup.

At the time, I was in my twenties and feeling pretty healthy. Besides, I thought sickness only attacked older people. After that message, the Holy Spirit kept bringing that message to mind. I probably had not had a checkup since my follow up when my first child was born about seven years earlier. I just remember my gut feeling, which I now know as the Holy Spirit kept prompting me to get a checkup. Since the Holy Spirit would not leave me alone, I made and went to the appointment. The doctor said everything looked fine, but he would check blood work and other tests.

A few days later I not only got a call I got a call from the doctor himself requesting I call his office. Included in the message were these words, "please contact my office right away?" that did not sit very well in my soul at first.

I made the call soon as I got the message. I spoke with the nurse who said the doctor was with a patient, but he would leave the patient to take my call. That really wasn't sounding good. He came to the phone with a calm voice explaining to me that my test revealed carcinoma in situ of the uterus. I was in the first stages of cancer of the uterus. The doctor asked me to come back for a scheduled surgery. I went to the scheduled surgery. All of the cancer cells were removed, and for several years, I was being tested every six months to make sure the cancer did not return.

It should have been more of a scary situation, but I had a peace I can't explain. All I know is during that shadow, the devil would whisper to me, "you are going to die" however I felt I wasn't. I did not fear the evil that tried to arrest me in fear because I knew My Shepherd was with me. I knew his rod, and his staff comforted me. His mighty strong hand held my hand every step of the way. The good Shepherd was watching over me. Sometimes I stop and think what if the good Shepherd had not sent the message I heard through the pastor that day where would I be. I don't believe in coincidences when it comes to life events like that, especially considering how the Holy Spirit strongly spoke to me about scheduling a checkup. My Shephard rescued me when I did not know I needed to be rescued because He watches over me.

Currently, I am experiencing a rough valley. My dad is presently ill, and hospice has been called in. They have tried to encourage our family by saying that they are not there to assist my dad in dying. However, with his age, medical condition, and him being weak to the point he no longer can get up on his own. We understand it's not but a matter of time apart from a miracle, the result will be his death, And as it is appointed unto men once to die (Hebrews 9:27a).

What gives me comfort is my dad saying that he trusts God, that God knows what is best for him. He said that he is weak and trying his best, but God knows when he is too tired, he will take him home to be with him. That says to me even in death, it is only a shadow because my dad and I know that God will take him home, not to just the dirt in the ground. He will go to his new home in heaven, where he will live again. His death is only a shadow. While his body will die (sleep), his spirit still lives.

> *Behold, I shew you a mystery; We shall not all sleep, but we shall all be changed, 52 In a moment, in the twinkling of an eye, at the last trump: for*

> *the trumpet shall sound, and the dead shall be raised incorruptible, and we shall be changed.*
>
> 1 Corinthians 15:51-52 (KJV)

Death has no power over him to keep him. He will end up in heaven, where sickness and diseases will no longer be a part of him. He will meet the good Shepherd, who, like dad, said, "He knows what is best for me." I am not looking forward to that day. I can't imagine life without him because I have known him all of my life. One thing for sure our Shepard is with him, and He is with me because his rod and his staff comfort him, and they comfort me. I will not be afraid of the shadow of death.

As I pick this book back up, I realize the time had come and gone. It was late one-night early morning on October 3, 2017, when my father went home to be with the Lord. My family and I, while we grieved as we should, we were prepared. We understood it was his time to leave this earth but not leave us forever. We knew he would be with the good Shepherd, who had watched over one of his sheep. Because the Lord is a good Shepherd, He came and rescued my father, who had begun to suffer tremendously. He will no longer experience pain, suffering, and he will get a new body. How exciting is that? He did not have to be afraid of the shadow that comes with dying. He did not have to fear death because it had no power over him, and it has no power or sting over us. There is nothing we should be afraid of, not even death or the threat of death because the Lord, our Shepherd, is in control of our dying. Dying is a part of life. We die daily, but we also die to live again. It is only a shadow that looks like the end. The scripture tells us,

> *Blessed are the dead which die in the Lord from henceforth: Yea, saith the Spirit, that they may rest from their labours; and their works do follow them*
> *Revelations 14:13*

My father walked through the valley of a shadow of death. It looked like he was gone forever. However, those of us who know the Lord, our Shepherd, knows it was just a shadow. Rest in heaven, dad. I will see you again one day soon.

5

WHAT DO YOU DO WITH YOUR ENEMIES?

Enjoy Lunch with Them

Thou preparest a table before me in the presence of mine enemies: thou anointest my head with oil; my cup runneth over.
Psalm 23:5

Did you know we all have enemies? We have lots of them. Even if we do not see them, they do exist. We have those enemies that smile in our face, but when we are not looking, they are stabbing us in our back. There is an old song called them backstabbers. Enemies do not necessarily use real knives to stab you in the back. They use words, negative actions, and in the spirit (unseen) realm; anything can be happening. The enemy's job is but for to steal, and to kill, and to destroy (John 10:10). The enemy wants to cause so much hurt and pain that will eventually destroy you. Sometimes we don't know what our enemies are doing, but our Shepherd does. He watches over us. We can understand if we ask the good Shepherd for discernment. Those who have a relationship with the Lord our Shepherd can sense when someone or something is not for us.

The enemy does not always come in the form of a person. It can come in the form of sickness, debt, and or worldly disaster or even come as a demonic force, principality, or rulers of darkness. In any case, if it comes to cause us harm, it is considered an enemy.

Most hostile enemies we encounter will come through a person influenced by the enemy who is Satan. But I must share an important truth; everything is not the devil.

Sometimes people are just evil. The good news is our enemies will never be greater than our Shepherd and never greater than us because,

> *Ye are of God, little children, and*
> *have overcome them: because*
> *greater is he that is in you,*
> *than he that is in the world*
> *(1John 4:4).*

Therefore, there is no need to fear our enemies; neither is there reason to fight our enemies, especially with physical weapons.

> *For the weapons of our warfare*
> *are not carnal, but mighty*
> *through God to the pulling*
> *down of strong holds;*
> 2 Corinthians 4:10

We can use the sword of the spirit, which is the word of God, and use praise to our God our Shepherd as a weapon. We can sit down and have lunch at the table with our enemies because the Lord, our Shepherd, has prepared the table for us. He has gone before us while the enemy is plotting to harm us. We can relax knowing that we are in good company at the Lord's table. Please don't forget the Lord Our Shepherd is at the table. He is paying attention to feeding and caring for his sheep. I like what the NIV Application Commentary says about being a guest at one's table as it relates to Psalm 23:5

To accept another as a guest at one's table was to set aside enmity and to assume responsibility for the safety of the guest while in your dwelling. To sit at Yahweh's table is to enjoy fellowship and communion with him. To do so "in the presence of my enemies" is to have one's special relationship to God declared publicly in a context of divine blessing and security.

Yes, we can feel blessed and secure when we come to the table with our enemies. The prophet Isaiah says,

> *No weapon that is formed against*
> *thee shall prosper; and every*

> *tongue that shall rise against thee in judgment thou shalt condemn. This is the heritage of the servants of the LORD, and their righteousness is of me, saith the LORD*
>
> *Isaiah 54:17 KJV*

I am encouraged to eat at the table that the Lord, my Shepherd, has prepared for me, right in the presence of my enemy. I know He is protecting me and keeping me from harm. How about you? Think about it? We can feast off of a good meal in the good company of the Shepherd. We can enjoy our lunch while the enemy is trying to plot and take us out. We do not have to fight or fear the enemy and his devices because when the Shepherd overcame, we overcame too. John 16:33 in the Amplified says,

> *I have told you these things, so that in Me you may have perfect peace and confidence. In the world you have*

> *tribulation and trial and distress and frustration; but be of good cheer take courage; be confident, certain, undaunted! For I have overcome the world. I have deprived it of power to harm you and have conquered it for you.*

Our Shepherd has deprived the enemy of the power of harming us. He has prepared great things for his children and has prepared blessings right in front of our enemies. So have lunch. Do something even greater. Love your enemies, as Matthew 5:44 instructs us to do.

> *But I say unto you, Love your enemies, bless them that curse you, do good to them that hate you, and pray for them which despitefully use you, and persecute you; Matthew5:44*

I often tell of how the enemy was trying to

get in the way of a promise my Shepherd had given me. My Shepherd had promised me a certain job. However, those who were in authority told me yes then sided with someone who decided for whatever reason to say no. I knew what the Lord my Shepherd had told me. I prayed and asked my Shepherd, who knew all things to open the door to the promise he had given me and to deal with those who were stopping me. It wasn't long before the two were gone. They both had to leave the company. They were replaced by others that came in that said yes to what the Shepherd had promised me. What was I doing in the meantime? I went to lunch. Most of my lunches consist of spiritual food such as prayer and fasting, but it got me to where my Shepherd promised me. Therefore, I encourage you to have lunch, even if you must go with your enemies.

> *Our Scriptures tell us that if you see your enemy hungry, go buy that person lunch, or if he's thirsty, get him a drink.*

Your generosity will surprise him with goodness. Don't let evil get the best of you; get the best of evil by doing good
Romans 12:2-22 TMB

6

GOODNESS AND MERCY WILL FOLLOW YOU

Surely goodness and mercy shall follow me all the days of my life: and I will dwell in the house of the LORD for ever.
Psalm 23:6

When I look at the definition of mercy, it is compassionate treatment from one who has the power to inflict harm. All I can see is what the Shepherd has shown me. When I deserve judgment, he shows me mercy. When I should have died for my sin, the good Shepherd sent his only Son to pay a horrible price for my sins. He died for me.

> *But God commendeth his love toward us, in that, while we were yet sinners, Christ died for us*
> Romans 5:8

I mean, he died a horrible death for my sins, for there are many. To my embarrassment, and sadly to say, even after I received forgiveness for my sins, I did not stop sinning. I try to live a good godly life daily. However, I still failed God by something I said or something I did. Before you judge me, the last time I checked the scripture says,

> *For all have sinned and come short the glory of God,*
> Romans 3:23

No deadly judgment. That is where God's mercy shines the most. While God did not give me or you a license to sin, there is grace and mercy for when we do and repent. One area that I tend to struggle with is when I am admonished to forgive those that genuinely cause me emotional pain. I don't get it how sometimes people can be so insensitive. I tend to think of myself as pretty loyal to those I allow to get close to me and share my life. Even when there is not a close connection, I believe in treating people right. However, that is not always returned. I don't believe people always mean to do hurtful things. Yet the pain of disappointment, especially from the people I love and trust, can be challenging for me. I think I can do the forgiveness part one or two times on my own. I have a problem with that seventy times seven that Jesus gave us an example in Matthew 18:21-22.

> *Then came Peter to him, and said, Lord, how oft shall my brother sin against me, and I forgive him? till seven times? Jesus saith unto him, I say not unto thee, Until seven times: but, Until seventy times seven.*

When I first read that, I thought surely the Shepherd is kidding. The Shepherd was just playing around. However, if you know anything about the Lord, our Shepherd, joking was not done often even though I believe He has a sense of humor. Therefore, I knew that when the Lord Jesus answered forgiveness to Peter, he was serious about what he said. He reminded me that all things are possible as I pondered on how this could be done when dealing with difficult and unlovable people. Most of all, he reminded me of how many times he has forgiven me without bringing things up again. Yes, that sin that he removes as far as the east is from the west. This is what real mercy following you looks like,

> *For as the heaven is high above the earth, so great is his mercy toward them that fear him. As far as the east is from the west, so far hath he removed our transgressions from us*
> Psalm 103:11-12

I am grateful that the good Shepherd has forgiven me, and Jesus died for all the stuff that I have done over the years. It is good that when I am struggling with forgiveness that God reminds me of his grace and mercy towards me. It is still following me, and it is there to cover me when I need it. By the way, I need it daily. When I am reminded of Shepherd's mercy, it helps me to forgive. That does not mean forgiveness is always easy but knowing the truth about what the Lord my Shepherd has done for me helps me. It is incredible how, when looking in the mirror at my own stuff, it tends to shine a light on how wretched I can be. I don't mind seeing my sin because it keeps me humble. I can make the corrections so that I can forgive and offer up the same mercy to others. Well, I try to get close to what the Shepherd has given me. The fact that his mercy follows me without me, even asking, is a blessing. Sometimes I will go there thinking I got it all together, not knowing how much mercy I need. But mercy is right there following me ready to show compassion when I need it most.

When using the word mercy, you can interchange the word with favor. That is why I want to do what is right because it shows the mercy of God in another way. I truly believe as I am writing this book; it is because the favor of the Lord surrounds me as a shield (Psalm 5:12). I believe that goodness and mercy follows me all the days of my life. Why wouldn't I want to dwell in the house of the Lord forever? You may ask, why do I think that I have so much favor? Well, when I show up to a job that I know I don't deserve, not that I don't work hard, and I am very passionate about what I do.

When it comes to this world's system, being in management, being a black female is not always on the top of the promotion list. Like I said earlier, I know who opened the door for me. I know it was the Shepherd's favor that caused me to be promoted. I have excellent supervision. That is another act of God's favor. If someone had told me ten years ago that I would be in this position, I would not have believed them because, at first, I did not believe God.

There was a prophetic word given to me years ago about me being in management. I thought the messenger had missed it because I did not believe I was management material. I did not want to be in management. I still am not crazy about it. However, God saw something he put in me that I did not see, favor. Goodness and mercy will allow you to be in places you and others think you are not qualified for. The good thing is the good Shepherd knows how to qualify you when he calls you,

> *Faithful is he that calleth you,*
> *who also will do it*
> *1 Thessalonians 5:24*

God's goodness and mercy is the favor of our good Shepherd following us wherever we go. It will chase us down if we confess it and believe it. The favor of God is looking for someone saying what they believe about the favor of the Shepherd. That is called a declaration of faith. If you believe you have favor, you should declare and decree it like you have it. I have added the declaration of favor that I use to declare and decree God's goodness and mercy (favor) over my life. It was inspired by one of the greatest preacher/teachers I know of in the world today, Dr. Bill Winston. I typed this declaration as a result of listening to his teaching on the favor of God. I would like to share this declaration with you:

THE FAVOR OF THE LORD

I declare and decree the favor of the Lord God surrounds me as shield:

"Surely, LORD, you bless the righteous; you surround them with your favor as with a shield." (Psalm 5:12 NIV)

Therefore:

> *I expect favor with God and man*
> *Luke 2:52, Ps 5:12*
>
> *I expect favor in my home and*
> *with family Ps 112:3*
>
> *I expect favor with my friends*

and relationships proverbs
18:24

I expect favor in my church
Hebrews 10:25

I expect favor on my job and in
my finances (give it comes
back) Luke 6:33

I expect favor when I shop, make
purchases, and make minor
and major decisions. Psalm
5:12

I expect debt cancellation (I'm in
constant Jubilee). Leviticus 25
12-13

I expect favor in my health (I
don't accept sickness and
disease) because, by His
stripes, I am already healed. 1
Peter 2:24

> *I expect petitions granted and miracles to happen when I pray (I have what I say in Jesus Name). Mark 11:23-24*
>
> *I expect miracles when I praise (Praise ye the LORD. O give thanks unto the LORD; for he is good: for his mercy endureth for ever Psalm 106:1)*
>
> *I expect wealth and riches to be in my house Psalm 112:3*

That means I expect: welfare, prosperity, good. Large possessions; a comparative abundance of things which are objects of human desire; esp., abundance of worldly estate, affluence (a flow to or towards) opulence (wealth riches and affluence) and riches (that which make one rich; an abundance of land, goods, money, and property). These are all definitions of wealth and riches.

I expect his goodness and mercy to follow me all the days of my life because He is a good Shepherd. I know the Lord my Shepherd watches over me. How about you? Wouldn't you like goodness and mercy to follow you all the days of your life? That promise can be yours. Will you allow the good Shepherd to take care of you? Will you let the Shepherd watch over you? He wants to watch over and take care of because that's what Shepherd's do. If this is what you want, all you have to do is repeat out loud this simple prayer:

> Father God, in the name of your Son Jesus Christ, I confess that I am a sinner, and I am in need of a savior. Therefore I repent of my sins known and unknown. I ask you to forgive me of all of my sins past and present and cleanse me of all unrighteousness. I confess with my mouth, and I believe with my heart that you died on the cross and that God has raised you from the dead so that I could be saved. Therefore I invite you to come into my life as my Lord and Savior. I invite into my life to be my Shepherd so that I will

not be in need. Thank you, Lord, in Jesus' Name. Amen!

Scripture References:

For all have sinned, and come short of the glory of God;
Romans 3:23

If we confess our sins, he is faithful and just to forgive us our sins, and to cleanse us from all unrighteousness.
1 John 1:9

That if thou shalt confess with thy mouth the Lord Jesus, and shalt believe in thine heart that God hath raised him from the dead, thou shalt be saved.
Romans 10:9-10

The LORD is my Shepherd; I shall not want.
Psalm 23:1

If you have prayed that simple yet powerful prayer, I would like to be the first to welcome you into the family of the good Shepherd. He loves you and longs to be with you, especially in times of trouble. I love Him. He has been good to me and has met and supplied all of my needs. Yes, I will forever trust Him because the Lord is my Shepherd. I have everything I need.

ABOUT THE AUTHOR

Carolyn Booker Pierce is a licensed social worker, teacher, mentor, and spiritual leader born and raised in Columbus, Ohio.

After leaving a career of almost 20 years in accounts payable and claims auditing, Carolyn followed her passion in the area of social services. She then graduated with a BA at Capital University to become a licensed social worker. Carolyn gravitates to chemical dependency counseling as a substance abuse group and individual counselor.

Later she took her years of experience as a substance abuse counselor into her local county jail to serve inmates struggling with substance abuse, alcoholism, and family relationship problems. She is known for listening to others without judgment as they process their everyday life problems.

Carolyn desires to help people grow, heal from their past, and move on to a healthy future. She enjoys spending time with her family, church worship center, traveling, writing, and empowering others.

facebook.com/carolyn.pierce.5245

ALSO BY CAROLYN BOOKER-PIERCE

Girl, You're Not Crazy. You're Dealing With a Narcissist

www.ingramcontent.com/pod-product-compliance
Lightning Source LLC
Chambersburg PA
CBHW052117110526
44592CB00013B/1644